Sportify

Jake Shannon
Sportify

All rights reserved
Copyright © 2023 by Jake Shannon

No part of this publication may be reproduced, distributed, or transmitted in any form or by any means, including photocopying, recording, or other electronic or mechanical methods, without the prior written permission of the publisher, except in the case of brief quotations embodied in critical reviews and certain other noncommercial uses permitted by copyright law.

Published by BooxAi

ISBN: 978-965-578-219-6

Sportify

Sportify Your Business: Unlocking the Power of Sports to Transform Your Organization

Jake Shannon

Contents

Introduction ix

Part One
The Foundations of Sportifying

1. THE POWER OF SPORTS: HOW SPORTS PRINCIPLES IMPACT BUSINESS PERFORMANCE 3
   Real-World Examples of Sports-Inspired Businesses 3
   Research on the Benefits of Sports Principles in a Business Context. 4

2. UNDERSTANDING SPORTIFYING: KEY CONCEPTS AND PRINCIPLES 6

3. THE SPORTIFIED COMPANY: CHARACTERISTICS AND BENEFITS 10
   Characteristics of Sportified Companies 10
   Case Studies of Successful Sportified Companies. 11
   Quantifiable Benefits of Sportifying in the Business World. 12

Part Two
Sportifying Your Business

4. IMPLEMENTING PHYSICALITY: BOOSTING EMPLOYEE HEALTH AND PRODUCTIVITY 17
   Strategies and Best Practices for Integrating Physical Activity in the Workplace 17
   The Impact of Employee Health on Productivity and Engagement. 18

5. FOSTERING TEAMWORK: BUILDING A COLLABORATIVE AND HIGH-PERFORMING CULTURE 20
   Effective Team-Building Activities and Initiatives ... 20
   The Importance of Communication and Collaboration in Business Success. 21

6. CULTIVATING SPORTSMANSHIP: ETHICAL LEADERSHIP AND WORKPLACE CULTURE ... 23
   Strategies for Promoting Fairness, Integrity and Respect. 23
   The Role of Ethical Leadership in Creating a Positive Work Environment. 24

7. DEVELOPING SKILLS: EMPOWERING EMPLOYEES THROUGH LEARNING AND GROWTH 26
   Implementing Training and Development Programs that Support Skill Development ... 26
   The Role of Continuous Learning in Employee Retention and Satisfaction 27

8. ENCOURAGING COMPETITION: DRIVING PERFORMANCE THROUGH HEALTHY RIVALRY 29
   Establishing Contests, Events and Recognition Systems that Promote Competition ... 29
   The Benefits of Competition in Motivating Employees: 30

9. ADAPTIVE DIFFICULTY: PERSONALIZING CHALLENGES FOR MAXIMUM ENGAGEMENT 32
   Techniques for Tailoring Challenges to Individual Employees' Skills and Abilities ... 32
   The Impact of Adaptive Difficulty on Employee Engagement and Performance: ... 33

10. COACHING AND MENTORSHIP: THE POWER
    OF GUIDANCE IN BUSINESS SUCCESS ... 35
    The Role and Importance of Coaching in a
    Business Context ... 35
    Strategies for Implementing Coaching and
    Mentorship Programs: ... 36
    Sportifying - Integrating Gamification and
    Coaching for Sustainable Motivation ... 37

11. PERSONALIZATION: CREATING UNIQUE
    EMPLOYEE EXPERIENCES ... 41
    Approaches to Customizing Employee
    Experiences Based on Preferences and Goals ... 41
    The Impact of Personalization on Employee
    Satisfaction and Loyalty ... 42

12. RECOGNITION AND REWARDS:
    CELEBRATING ACHIEVEMENTS AND
    MILESTONES ... 44
    Effective Systems for Recognizing and
    Rewarding Employee Accomplishments ... 44
    The Influence of Recognition and Rewards on
    Employee Motivation ... 45

13. SPECTATORSHIP: LEARNING AND GROWING
    THROUGH OBSERVATION ... 47
    Opportunities for Employees to Observe and
    Learn from Their Colleagues ... 47
    The Role of Spectatorship in Fostering a
    Supportive and Inspired Workplace ... 48

Part Three
The Sportified Company Certification and NoI Coaching

14. THE SPORTIFIED COMPANY
    CERTIFICATION: A COMPETITIVE
    ADVANTAGE ... 51
    Overview of the Certification Process and
    Criteria ... 51
    Benefits of Becoming a Certified Sportified
    Company ... 52

15. NO1 COACHING: YOUR PARTNER IN
    SPORTIFYING 54
    Introduction to No1 Coaching and its Services
    and Products 54
    How No1 Coaching Can Help Organizations
    Achieve Sportifying and the Sportified Company
    Certification 55

16. CONCLUSION - THE FUTURE OF
    SPORTIFYING AND THE ROLE OF NO1
    COACHING 57
    The Future of *Sportifying* in the Business World 57
    The Role of No1 Coaching in Driving the
    Sportifying Movement 58

Appendix 1: Conceptual Upgrades and Scaling
Through Sportifying 61
Appendix 2– The Sportified Company
Certification Program 67
Bibliography 73

Introduction

In today's rapidly evolving business landscape, organizations are continuously seeking new ways to enhance performance, employee engagement, and overall success. As a result, various approaches to improving organizational culture and employee development have emerged. One such innovative approach is the concept of *Sportifying*, which draws on the power of sports to transform businesses and unlock their full potential. This book, *Sportify Your Business: Unlocking the Power of Sports to Transform Your Organization*, delves into the principles of *Sportifying* and showcases how businesses can apply these principles to achieve a competitive advantage and foster a high-performing culture.

The idea of *Sportifying* revolves around the integration of elements from sports into the business world, leveraging the proven benefits of sports principles to enhance employee performance, motivation, and well-being (Kim, Williams, & Rothstein, 2013). By incorporating aspects such as teamwork, competition, skill development, coaching and mentorship, personalization, and physical activity into the workplace, businesses can create an environment that encourages growth, collaboration and continuous improvement (Sailer, Hense, Mandl, & Klevers, 2013).

As pioneers in the field of *Sportifying*, No1 Coaching has played an instrumental role in developing and promoting this groundbreaking approach. Through our research, training programs and consulting services, we have helped countless organizations implement Sportifying strategies and achieve remarkable results. Our success in the field has not only established No1 Coaching as the leader in *Sportifying* but has also led to the development of the *Sportified Company Certification*, a prestigious recognition for organizations that successfully adopt and embody the principles of *Sportifying*.

I came to many of these conclusions while simultaneously coaching both C-Suite executives via No1 Coaching and high-level combat sports athletes via Scientific Wrestling. I see *Sportifying* as the winner in the ultimate battle between intrinsic motivation and extrinsic motivation when you contrast the world of Western-style combat sports like boxing and wrestling with the more Eastern-influenced martial art belt systems. Get ready to rumble!

Deci and Ryan's Self-determination Theory identifies three essential elements of intrinsic motivation: competence, autonomy and relatedness (Ryan, R. M., & Deci, E. L., 2000). These factors make activities enjoyable, meaningful, and engaging in and of themselves, without the need for any external rewards.

Western Combat Sports: The Intrinsic Motivation Heavyweights.

Boxing and wrestling are perfect examples of activities that embody these three elements:

1. Competence: These sports focus on developing skills, strength and strategy, providing a sense of accomplishment as participants progress and overcome challenges (Pink, D. H., 2009).
2. Autonomy: Athletes have the freedom to choose their training methods, techniques and even their opponents in competitions, ensuring that they feel in control of their journey.
3. Relatedness: The sense of camaraderie and shared goals in these sports foster connections with teammates, coaches, and the broader athletic community.

Intrinsic motivation thrives in the realm of Western combat sports, as athletes push themselves to achieve their personal bests, not because of external rewards but for the love of the sport.

Martial Arts Belt System: The Extrinsic Motivation Contender.

On the other hand, the martial arts belt system is primarily based on extrinsic motivators, such as rank and status (Rigby, S., & Ryan, R. M., 2011). Although it can provide a sense of accomplishment and progression, the focus on external rewards may hinder the development of intrinsic motivation.

The Winner: Combat Sports or Martial Arts?

Research has shown that intrinsic motivation is more powerful and effective than extrinsic motivation (Deci, E. L., Koestner, R., & Ryan, R. M.,1999). By focusing on the love of the sport rather than external rewards like belts or ranks, Western combat sports foster a more sustainable and enjoyable experience for athletes.

In conclusion, the intrinsic motivation training methods of Western combat sports triumph over the extrinsic motivation of the martial arts belt system. Whether you're a seasoned athlete or a beginner, embracing intrinsic motivation will take your performance to new heights and ensure that you truly love the journey.

In the following chapters, we will explore the foundations of *Sportifying*, its key concepts and principles and how they can be applied to your business. We will provide practical strategies, real-world examples and research-based insights to help you transform your organization and achieve unparalleled success. Furthermore, we will introduce you to No1 Coaching's comprehensive suite of products and services designed to support your *Sportifying* journey, including our flagship offering, the Sportified Company Certification.

Join us as we unlock the power of sports and *Sportifying*, enabling you to revolutionize your business, enhance employee engagement, and create a lasting competitive edge.

Part One

The Foundations of Sportifying

Chapter 1

The Power of Sports: How Sports Principles Impact Business Performance

Sports have long been recognized for their ability to inspire, motivate and bring people together in the pursuit of common goals. From the discipline and determination of individual athletes to the camaraderie and teamwork of championship-winning teams, the principles of sports can be powerful catalysts for success. It should come as no surprise, then, that many businesses have begun to recognize the potential of incorporating sports principles into their operations to drive performance and achieve outstanding results.

Real-World Examples of Sports-Inspired Businesses

Numerous organizations have successfully integrated sports principles into their business strategies and reaped the benefits. For example, Google's work culture is renowned for its emphasis on employee well-being, collaboration, and innovation (Bock, 2015). The company's campus features sports facilities such as gyms, basketball courts and swimming pools, promoting physical activity and fostering a sense of camaraderie among employees. This sports-inspired approach has contributed to Google's consistently high rankings in employee satisfaction surveys and its reputation as one of the best places to work.

Another example is the corporate culture at Nike, where the company's sports heritage and "Just Do It" mentality permeates all aspects of the organization (Edwards, 2019). Employees are encouraged to adopt a performance-driven mindset, embrace competition, and continuously strive for personal and professional growth. This sports-inspired ethos has enabled Nike to become a global powerhouse in the athletic apparel industry and maintain a strong internal culture that attracts top talent.

Research on the Benefits of Sports Principles in a Business Context.

There is a growing body of research highlighting the positive impact of sports principles on business performance. For instance, a study by Kim, Williams, and Rothstein (2013) found that organizations that implemented sports-based interventions reported improvements in workplace well-being, employee engagement, and overall performance. The study also revealed that such interventions fostered a sense of teamwork and collaboration, resulting in a more cohesive and high-performing work environment.

Similarly, Sailer, Hense, Mandl, and Klevers (2013) explored the psychological effects of incorporating sports principles into the workplace, focusing on the motivational aspects of *Sportifying*. Their findings suggest that businesses that successfully integrate sports-inspired elements, such as competition, goal-setting, and skill development, can experience significant improvements in employee motivation, engagement, and performance.

The research clearly demonstrates that incorporating sports principles into business operations can lead to numerous benefits, including higher employee satisfaction, increased productivity and improved overall performance. As more organizations recognize the power of *Sportifying* and begin to adopt these principles, it becomes increasingly apparent that the sports world has much to offer the business community.

In the coming chapters, we will delve deeper into the specific principles of *Sportifying* and explore how your business can harness the power of sports to revolutionize your organization and drive success.

Chapter 2

Understanding Sportifying: Key Concepts and Principles

Sportifying is a multifaceted approach to business that draws inspiration from the world of sports to create a high-performing, engaging, and fulfilling work environment. By understanding and implementing the key concepts and principles of *Sportifying*, organizations can harness the power of sports to transform their operations and achieve unparalleled success. In this chapter, we will explore the ten core principles of *Sportifying* and their potential impact on businesses.

1. Physicality

Physical activity plays a crucial role in maintaining overall health and well-being and incorporating physicality into the workplace can lead to numerous benefits, such as increased productivity, reduced stress and improved employee satisfaction (Pronk, 2015). Examples of promoting physicality in the workplace include providing fitness facilities, encouraging walking meetings and offering wellness programs that support employee health.

2. Teamwork

Effective teamwork is essential for organizational success, fostering collaboration, communication, and problem-solving skills (Salas, Cooke, & Rosen, 2008). Businesses can cultivate teamwork by creating opportunities for team-based projects, organizing team-building activities, and emphasizing the importance of cooperation and shared goals.

3. Sportsmanship

Sportsmanship encompasses the values of respect, fairness, and integrity, all of which contribute to a positive and ethical work environment. Companies can promote sportsmanship by establishing clear policies and guidelines for ethical behavior, providing training on conflict resolution and modeling respectful interactions among employees and leaders.

4. Skill Development

Continuous learning and skill development are vital for employee growth, engagement, and retention (Noe, Clarke, & Klein, 2014). Organizations can support skill development by offering training programs, workshops and other learning opportunities that align with employee interests and organizational goals.

5. Competition

Healthy competition can be a powerful motivator, driving employees to push themselves and excel in their work (Kohn, 1992). To encourage competition, companies can create contests, events, and recognition systems that reward high performance and innovation.

6. Adaptive Difficulty

Adaptive difficulty involves tailoring challenges to individual employees' abilities and goals, ensuring that tasks are engaging and appropriately challenging (Gagné & Deci, 2005). Businesses can achieve adaptive difficulty by implementing systems that account for employees' skills, strengths, and preferences, allowing for personalized goal-setting and task allocation.

7. Coaching and Mentorship

Coaching and mentorship are essential for supporting employee development and fostering a culture of continuous learning (Hagen, 2012). Companies can establish formal coaching and mentorship programs, pairing experienced employees with less experienced colleagues to provide guidance, support and knowledge sharing.

8. Personalization

Personalization involves customizing employee experiences based on individual preferences, abilities and aspirations (Anaza & Rutherford, 2012). Businesses can personalize employee experiences by offering flexible work arrangements, tailoring development opportunities, and providing individualized feedback and support.

9. Recognition and Rewards

Recognizing and rewarding employee achievements and milestones are crucial for maintaining motivation and engagement (Gagné & Deci, 2005). Companies can establish systems that acknowledge accomplishments, celebrate progress and provide tangible rewards for exceptional performance.

10. Spectatorship

Spectatorship refers to the opportunities for employees to observe, learn from, and support the achievements of their colleagues, fostering a sense of community and inspiration. Businesses can promote spectatorship by hosting events that showcase employee accomplishments, creating spaces for knowledge sharing and encouraging cross-departmental collaboration.

By understanding and implementing these core principles of *Sportifying*, organizations can harness the power of sports to create a high-performing, engaging and fulfilling work environment. In the following chapters, we will explore practical strategies and real-world examples to help you apply these principles in your organization and unlock your business.

Chapter 3

The Sportified Company: Characteristics and Benefits

As we have seen in the previous chapters, *Sportifying* is a powerful approach to enhancing business performance, employee engagement, and overall success. Organizations that embrace the principles of *Sportifying* are often characterized by a dynamic, growth-oriented culture, where employees are empowered to reach their full potential. In this chapter, we will explore the defining characteristics of sportified companies, examine case studies of successful organizations and delve into the quantifiable benefits of Sportifying in the business world.

Characteristics of Sportified Companies

Sportified companies share several key characteristics, which set them apart from their competitors and contribute to their overall success. These characteristics include:

1. A focus on employee well-being and physicality, with facilities and programs designed to promote health and fitness.

2. A strong emphasis on teamwork, collaboration and shared goals, creating a supportive and cohesive work environment.
3. A commitment to sportsmanship, ethical behavior and fairness, fostering a culture of respect and integrity.
4. Opportunities for continuous learning and skill development, encouraging personal and professional growth.
5. Healthy competition, driving employees to excel in their roles and contribute to organizational success.
6. Adaptive difficulty, with personalized challenges and goals tailored to individual abilities and aspirations.
7. Coaching and mentorship, supporting employee development and creating a culture of continuous improvement.
8. Personalization, ensuring employee experiences are customized to individual preferences, abilities and goals.
9. Recognition and rewards, acknowledging employee achievements and milestones and maintaining motivation and engagement.
10. Spectatorship, creating opportunities for employees to observe, learn from, and support the achievements of their colleagues.

Case Studies of Successful Sportified Companies.

1. Google: As mentioned in Chapter 1, Google is a prime example of a sportified company, with a strong emphasis on employee well-being, teamwork, and innovation (Bock, 2015). The company's sports-inspired culture has led to consistently high employee

satisfaction ratings and a reputation as one of the best places to work.
2. Nike: Nike's sports heritage and "Just Do It" mentality are deeply ingrained in the company's culture, with a focus on performance, competition, and personal growth (Edwards, 2019). This sports-inspired approach has helped Nike become a global leader in athletic apparel and maintain a strong internal culture that attracts top talent.

Quantifiable Benefits of Sportifying in the Business World.

Several studies have demonstrated the quantifiable benefits of *Sportifying* for businesses, including:

1. Improved employee well-being: Organizations that implement sports-based interventions report improvements in workplace well-being, reduced stress and increased job satisfaction (Kim, Williams, & Rothstein, 2013).
2. Increased employee engagement: Research has shown that companies that incorporate sports principles, such as competition, goal-setting and skill development, experience significant improvements in employee motivation, engagement, and performance (Sailer et al., 2013).
3. Enhanced productivity: Studies have found that physical activity and exercise can lead to increased productivity, reduced absenteeism and lower healthcare costs (Pronk, 2015).
4. Higher retention rates: Businesses that prioritize employee growth, skill development, and personalization tend to have higher retention rates, as

employees are more likely to feel valued, supported, and motivated to stay with the organization (Noe et al., 2014).

By understanding the characteristics and benefits of sportified companies, organizations can begin to harness the power of *Sportifying* to transform their operations and achieve unparalleled success. In the coming chapters, we will explore practical strategies and guidance for implementing *Sportifying* principles in your business, unlocking the full potential of your organization and employees.

Part Two

Sportifying Your Business

Chapter 4
Implementing Physicality: Boosting Employee Health and Productivity

Physical activity plays a crucial role in overall health, well-being and work performance. A growing body of evidence suggests that integrating physical activity into the workplace can lead to numerous benefits, such as increased productivity, reduced stress and improved employee satisfaction. In this chapter, we will explore strategies and best practices for incorporating physicality into your organization, as well as the impact of employee health on productivity and engagement.

Strategies and Best Practices for Integrating Physical Activity in the Workplace

1. Create a fitness-friendly environment: Design your workplace to encourage physical activity, such as providing on-site fitness facilities, standing desks, and dedicated spaces for stretching or meditation (Garrett et al., 2016).
2. Promote walking meetings: Encourage employees to conduct meetings while walking, either indoors or

outdoors. Walking meetings can boost creativity, improve mood and promote physical activity (Oppezzo & Schwartz, 2014).
3. Offer wellness programs: Develop comprehensive wellness programs that focus on physical activity, nutrition, stress management and other aspects of health. Research shows that well-designed wellness programs can lead to significant improvements in employee health and well-being (Baicker et al., 2010).
4. Encourage active commuting: Provide incentives for employees to bike, walk or use public transportation to get to work. Active commuting can help employees incorporate regular physical activity into their daily routines and has been linked to improved health outcomes (Hamer & Chida, 2008).
5. Organize sports teams and events: Establish company sports teams, organize recreational leagues or sponsor participation in local sports events. These initiatives can help build camaraderie and foster a culture of physical activity.

The Impact of Employee Health on Productivity and Engagement.

There is a strong connection between employee health and productivity, as healthier employees tend to be more engaged, less stressed and better able to focus on their work (Mills et al., 2007). Several studies have demonstrated the positive impact of physical activity and overall employee health on productivity and engagement, including:

1. Improved cognitive function: Regular physical activity has been shown to enhance cognitive

function, leading to better problem-solving, decision-making, and overall work performance (Hillman et al., 2008).
2. Reduced stress and burnout: Physical activity can help alleviate stress and prevent burnout, contributing to increased employee engagement and satisfaction (Pelletier, 2005).
3. Lower absenteeism: Active and healthy employees are less likely to take sick leaves, leading to reduced absenteeism and improved productivity (Pronk, 2015).
4. Enhanced creativity: Exercise has been found to boost creativity, potentially leading to more innovative ideas and solutions in the workplace (Oppezzo & Schwartz, 2014).

By implementing strategies to promote physical activity and overall employee health, organizations can unlock the benefits of increased productivity, engagement and satisfaction. In the next chapter, we will explore the importance of teamwork in sportified companies and discuss practical strategies for fostering a collaborative and cohesive work environment.

Chapter 5

Fostering Teamwork: Building a Collaborative and High-Performing Culture

Teamwork and collaboration are essential components of a successful organization, with numerous studies highlighting their importance for overall business performance, innovation and employee satisfaction. In this chapter, we will explore effective team-building activities and initiatives that can help create a collaborative and high-performing culture within your organization. Additionally, we will discuss the significance of communication and collaboration in achieving business success.

Effective Team-Building Activities and Initiatives

1. Team-building exercises: Engage in team-building exercises that promote collaboration, trust and problem-solving skills. These activities can include icebreakers, interactive games or simulations that challenge employees to work together toward a common goal (Klein et al., 2009).
2. Cross-functional collaboration: Encourage employees to work on projects with colleagues from different

departments, fostering an environment where diverse perspectives and skills are valued and utilized (Edmondson, 2012).
3. Group training and development: Offer group training sessions that focus on teamwork, communication and leadership skills, helping employees better understand and appreciate their colleagues' roles and contributions (Lacerenza et al., 2017).
4. Recognize team achievements: Celebrate and acknowledge the accomplishments of teams, reinforcing the importance of collaboration and shared success (Gostick & Elton, 2009).
5. Organize social events: Encourage employees to interact and bond outside of work through social events, sports activities or community service projects. These events can help build relationships and create a more cohesive team environment (Tews et al., 2013).

The Importance of Communication and Collaboration in Business Success.

Effective communication and collaboration are crucial for business success, as they facilitate efficient decision-making, problem-solving, and innovation. Research has shown that organizations with strong communication and collaboration practices experience numerous benefits, including:

1. Improved performance: Teams that communicate effectively and collaborate closely have been shown to achieve higher levels of performance and productivity (Salas et al., 2005).
2. Enhanced innovation: Collaborative work environments promote the exchange of ideas and

facilitate the development of innovative solutions to complex problems (Hülsheger et al., 2009).
3. Increased employee satisfaction: A positive and collaborative work culture can lead to increased employee satisfaction, as individuals feel more engaged, supported, and valued within their teams (Gallup, 2017).
4. Reduced turnover: Strong communication and collaboration can help to prevent misunderstandings, reduce conflict, and foster a sense of belonging, ultimately contributing to lower turnover rates (Griffeth et al., 2000).

By fostering teamwork and promoting a collaborative, high-performing culture, organizations can unlock the full potential of their employees and achieve lasting success. In the following chapters, we will explore additional Sportifying principles and provide practical guidance for implementing these concepts within your organization.

Chapter 6

Cultivating Sportsmanship: Ethical Leadership and Workplace Culture

Sportsmanship is an essential component of successful sports teams, as it fosters a culture of fairness, integrity, and respect among athletes. These same principles can be applied to the business world, as ethical leadership and strong workplace culture are vital for long-term success. In this chapter, we will explore strategies for promoting sportsmanship in the workplace and discuss the role of ethical leadership in creating a positive work environment.

Strategies for Promoting Fairness, Integrity and Respect.

1. Develop a clear code of conduct: Establish a comprehensive code of conduct that outlines the organization's values and expectations for employee behavior. This code should emphasize fairness, integrity and respect and serve as a guide for decision-making and conflict resolution (Treviño et al., 2014).

2. Provide ethics training: Offer regular training sessions on ethical decision-making, emphasizing the importance of upholding the organization's values and adhering to the code of conduct. This training can help employees better understand their ethical responsibilities and equip them with the tools to navigate challenging situations (Mayer et al., 2012).
3. Encourage open communication: Foster an environment where employees feel comfortable discussing ethical concerns, sharing ideas and providing feedback. Open communication can help promote fairness, as employees have an opportunity to voice their concerns and ensure that their perspectives are considered (Carmeli et al., 2009).
4. Recognize and reward ethical behavior: Acknowledge employees who demonstrate exceptional ethical behavior, providing incentives for others to follow suit. This recognition can take the form of public praise, promotions or other rewards that reinforce the importance of upholding the organization's values (Treviño et al., 2011).

The Role of Ethical Leadership in Creating a Positive Work Environment.

Ethical leadership plays a critical role in cultivating a positive work environment, as leaders set the tone for organizational culture and serve as role models for employees. Research has shown that ethical leadership is associated with numerous benefits, including:

1. Increased trust: Ethical leaders are more likely to foster trust among employees, which can contribute

to a strong sense of teamwork and collaboration (Dirks & Ferrin, 2002).
2. Enhanced employee engagement: Employees who perceive their leaders as ethical are more likely to feel engaged and committed to their work, as they believe that their efforts are valued and that the organization is operating with integrity (Den Hartog et al., 2013).
3. Reduced misconduct: Organizations with ethical leadership are less likely to experience instances of misconduct or unethical behavior, as employees are more inclined to adhere to the organization's values and code of conduct (Treviño et al., 2014).
4. Improved reputation: Ethical leadership can enhance the organization's reputation, both internally and externally, attracting top talent and promoting customer loyalty (Brammer et al., 2007).

By cultivating sportsmanship through ethical leadership and fostering a workplace culture based on fairness, integrity and respect, organizations can unlock the power of sports to transform their business and achieve long-term success.

Chapter 7

Developing Skills: Empowering Employees through Learning and Growth

Skill development is a fundamental aspect of sports, as athletes continuously hone their abilities to achieve peak performance. In the business world, empowering employees through learning and growth is equally important, as it contributes to both individual and organizational success. In this chapter, we will discuss the implementation of training and development programs that support skill development, as well as the role of continuous learning in employee retention and satisfaction.

Implementing Training and Development Programs that Support Skill Development

1. Assess employee needs: Conduct a thorough analysis of employee skills and knowledge to identify areas for improvement and growth. This assessment can include performance reviews, employee surveys or skills gap analyses (Noe et al., 2017).
2. Design customized training programs: Develop training programs tailored to the specific needs of

your employees, incorporating various learning methods such as workshops, e-learning modules and on-the-job training to accommodate different learning styles (Aguinis & Kraiger, 2009).
3. Foster a culture of learning: Create an environment that encourages continuous learning and development, providing employees with opportunities to take on new challenges, attend training sessions and learn from their peers (Marsick & Watkins, 2003).
4. Monitor progress and measure outcomes: Regularly evaluate the effectiveness of your training and development programs, gathering feedback from employees and tracking performance improvements to ensure that your initiatives are yielding positive results (Saks & Haccoun, 2010).

The Role of Continuous Learning in Employee Retention and Satisfaction

Continuous learning plays a significant role in employee retention and satisfaction, as it enables individuals to stay engaged, acquire new skills and advance their careers. Research has shown that organizations that prioritize employee learning and development experience numerous benefits, including:

1. Enhanced performance: Employees who engage in continuous learning are more likely to develop new skills and knowledge, leading to improved job performance and productivity (Tharenou et al., 2007).
2. Increased job satisfaction: Employees who have access to learning and development opportunities are more likely to feel satisfied with their jobs, as they

perceive their organization as invested in their personal and professional growth (Maurer, 2001).
3. Improved retention: Offering ongoing learning and development opportunities can contribute to reduced turnover, as employees are more likely to remain with organizations that support their growth and development (Noe, 1999).
4. Attracting top talent: Organizations that prioritize employee learning and development are more likely to attract high-performing candidates who value professional growth and development (Nyberg et al., 2010).

By implementing effective training and development programs and fostering a culture of continuous learning, organizations can empower their employees, unlocking the power of sports to transform their businesses and achieve long-term success.

Chapter 8
Encouraging Competition: Driving Performance through Healthy Rivalry

Competition is an integral component of sports, as it drives athletes to push their limits and strive for excellence. In the business world, healthy competition can similarly fuel performance and inspire employees to reach their full potential. In this chapter, we will discuss how to establish contests, events and recognition systems that promote competition, as well as the benefits of competition in motivating employees.

Establishing Contests, Events and Recognition Systems that Promote Competition

1. Set clear goals and objectives: Define specific, measurable, achievable, relevant, and time-bound (SMART) goals for employees to encourage friendly competition and drive performance (Doran, 1981).
2. Organize contests and events: Host events or contests that encourage employees to compete against one another, such as sales competitions or innovation

challenges, to boost engagement and productivity (Kohn, 1992).
3. Implement performance-based rewards: Develop a recognition system that rewards employees for their achievements, such as bonuses, promotions, or public recognition, to motivate them to perform at their best (Cerasoli et al., 2014).
4. Promote transparency: Share performance metrics and progress updates with employees, fostering a sense of accountability and inspiring them to compete with their peers to improve their performance (Prendergast, 1999).

The Benefits of Competition in Motivating Employees:

When implemented effectively, competition can have numerous benefits in motivating employees, including:

1. Increased productivity: Friendly competition can inspire employees to work harder and more efficiently, ultimately boosting productivity (Murayama & Elliot, 2012).
2. Enhanced performance: Competing against peers can push employees to develop new skills and refine their existing ones, leading to improved job performance (Tauer & Harackiewicz, 2004).
3. Greater innovation: Competition can spark creativity and drive employees to develop innovative solutions, products or services that contribute to organizational success (Amabile et al., 1996).
4. Higher employee engagement: Competitive environments can foster a sense of excitement and engagement among employees, as they strive to

outperform their peers and achieve their goals (Meyer et al., 2004).

By encouraging competition through contests, events and recognition systems, organizations can harness the power of healthy rivalry to drive performance and transform their business.

Chapter 9

Adaptive Difficulty: Personalizing Challenges for Maximum Engagement

In sports, adaptive difficulty is a key aspect of training and development, as it ensures that athletes are consistently challenged at the appropriate level to foster growth and improvement. In a business context, personalizing challenges to suit individual employees' skills and abilities can lead to increased engagement and enhanced performance. In this chapter, we will explore techniques for tailoring challenges to individual employees and discuss the impact of adaptive difficulty on employee engagement and performance.

Techniques for Tailoring Challenges to Individual Employees' Skills and Abilities

1. Conduct skills assessments: Regularly assess employee skills and abilities to identify areas of strength and weakness and use this information to create personalized challenges (Noe et al., 2017).
2. Set individual goals: Establish specific, measurable, achievable, relevant and time-bound (SMART)

goals for each employee, taking into account their unique skills and potential for growth (Doran, 1981).
3. Provide customized training: Offer tailored training and development programs that address individual employees' needs, helping them develop new skills and overcome specific challenges (Aguinis & Kraiger, 2009).
4. Implement flexible work assignments: Assign tasks and projects that are suited to employees' unique strengths and abilities, allowing them to take on challenges that are both engaging and achievable (Humphrey et al., 2007).

The Impact of Adaptive Difficulty on Employee Engagement and Performance:

Adaptive difficulty has been shown to have a positive impact on employee engagement and performance, as it ensures that employees are consistently challenged and motivated to improve. Benefits of adaptive difficulty include:

1. Increased engagement: When employees are challenged at the appropriate level, they are more likely to feel engaged and invested in their work (Kahn, 1990).
2. Enhanced performance: Personalized challenges that are tailored to employees' skills and abilities can lead to improved performance, as they are more likely to be motivated to overcome obstacles and achieve their goals (Locke & Latham, 2002).
3. Greater job satisfaction: Employees who experience adaptive difficulty in their work are more likely to feel satisfied with their jobs, as they perceive their

organization as committed to their personal and professional growth (Maurer, 2001).
4. Reduced turnover: Providing employees with tailored challenges can contribute to reduced turnover, as employees are more likely to remain with organizations that support their growth and development (Noe, 1999).

By implementing adaptive difficulty in the workplace, organizations can create an engaging and motivating environment that fosters employee growth and drives performance, ultimately unlocking the power of sports to transform their business.

Chapter 10

Coaching and Mentorship: The Power of Guidance in Business Success

Coaching and mentorship play a crucial role in the world of sports, helping athletes refine their skills, overcome challenges and reach their full potential. Similarly, in a business context, coaching and mentorship can have a significant impact on employee performance, job satisfaction, and overall success. In this chapter, we will discuss the role and importance of coaching in a business context, supported by data and explore strategies for implementing coaching and mentorship programs within organizations.

The Role and Importance of Coaching in a Business Context

Coaching and mentorship provide valuable support for employees in the following ways

1. Improved performance: Research has shown that coaching can lead to significant improvements in employee performance, with one meta-analysis

finding an average return on investment of 5.7 times the initial investment in coaching (McGill & Slocum, 1998; Parker-Wilkins, 2006).
2. Enhanced skills development: Coaching can help employees develop new skills and refine existing ones, contributing to their professional growth and the organization's overall success (de Haan et al., 2013).
3. Increased job satisfaction: Employees who receive coaching and mentorship are more likely to feel satisfied with their jobs and committed to their organizations (Eby et al., 2013).
4. Reduced turnover: Providing employees with coaching and mentorship can contribute to lower turnover rates, as they are more likely to stay with organizations that invest in their growth and development (Allen et al., 2004).

Strategies for Implementing Coaching and Mentorship Programs:

1. Assess employee needs: Identify the areas where employees require support and guidance and use this information to tailor coaching and mentorship programs to address specific needs (Noe et al., 2017).
2. Train and develop coaches: Provide training and development for managers and leaders within the organization, equipping them with the necessary skills to effectively coach and mentor their teams (Aguinis & Kraiger, 2009).
3. Establish clear goals and expectations: Set specific, measurable, achievable, relevant and time-bound (SMART) goals for both the coaching process and

desired outcomes, ensuring that all parties are aligned and working towards the same objectives (Doran, 1981).
4. Provide ongoing support and feedback: Ensure that coaches and mentors are available to provide regular feedback and support, helping employees stay on track and adjust their approach as needed (Rock & Donde, 2008).

By harnessing the power of coaching and mentorship, organizations can promote employee growth, drive performance, and unlock the transformative potential of sports in the business world.

Sportifying - Integrating Gamification and Coaching for Sustainable Motivation

The concept of *Sportifying* emerges as a novel solution to address the challenges of extrinsic motivation in gamification by combining it with the intrinsic solutions provided by coaching. This chapter explores the integration of gamification tools with professional coaching tools to create a transformative approach called *Sportifying*.

Gamification has been shown to drive engagement, motivation and performance in various settings (Deterding et al., 2011). However, relying solely on extrinsic rewards may lead to decreased motivation over time (Deci, Kasser, & Ryan, 1999). By integrating coaching tools that foster intrinsic motivation, *Sportifying* presents a sustainable approach to enhancing performance and personal growth.

To Sportify the coaching process, we can incorporate gamification elements into each of the coaching tools listed earlier:

1. Playbook: Include gamified elements such as progress bars, badges or levels that represent the client's advancement through the coaching program (Hamari, Koivisto, & Sarsa, 2014).
2. Assessment Tools: Enhance traditional assessments with game-like features, such as leaderboards, to encourage friendly competition and facilitate self-improvement (Morschheuser, Hamari, & Koivisto, 2016).
3. Goal Setting Templates: Integrate goal-setting with gamified milestones and rewards to celebrate achievements and maintain motivation (Seaborn & Fels, 2015).
4. Action Plans: Incorporate challenges or quests, offering points or badges upon completion, to keep clients engaged and focused on their objectives (Werbach & Hunter, 2012).
5. Monitoring and Tracking Tools: Use gamified progress indicators, such as experience points or level-ups, to visualize clients' growth and accomplishments (Koivisto & Hamari, 2019).
6. Coaching Session Agendas: Structure sessions around game-like objectives and strategies, fostering a sense of achievement and forward momentum (Landers, Auerbach, & Callan, 2017).
7. Journaling and Reflection Exercises: Integrate game mechanics, such as unlocking new content or earning rewards, to encourage regular reflection and self-awareness (Nicholson, 2015).
8. Visualization Techniques: Employ interactive storytelling or virtual reality simulations to enhance clients' ability to envision their desired outcomes (Kapp, 2012).

9. Feedback and Evaluation Forms: Incorporate feedback mechanisms from gaming, such as real-time analytics, to provide clients with actionable insights and facilitate continuous improvement (Farzan & Brusilovsky, 2011).
10. Networking and Resource Sharing: Create collaborative platforms where clients can engage in team-based challenges, share resources, and learn from one another (Zichermann & Cunningham, 2011).
11. Communication Platforms: Use game-like communication methods, such as avatars or virtual environments, to facilitate immersive and engaging interactions between coaches and clients (Nacke & Deterding, 2017).
12. Professional Development and Continuing Education: Encourage lifelong learning by offering gamified learning experiences, such as skill-based challenges or interactive workshops (Raybourn, 2014).
13. Online Learning Platforms: Integrate game elements into online courses and resources, promoting engagement and knowledge retention (Sailer, Hense, Mayr, & Mandl, 2017).
14. Mindfulness and Stress-Management Techniques: Utilize gamified meditation or relaxation apps to help clients develop healthy coping mechanisms and maintain balance (Roepke, Jaffee, Riffle, & McGonigal, 2015).

In conclusion, *Sportifying* combines the benefits of gamification and coaching to create a powerful approach for fostering sustainable motivation and personal growth. By integrating game elements with proven coaching tools, we can create a more engaging, rewarding and effective coaching experience that promotes intrinsic motivation and long-term success. This innovative approach has the potential to revolutionize the coaching industry, driving better outcomes for clients and organizations alike.

Chapter 11

Personalization: Creating Unique Employee Experiences

Just as sports teams tailor their training and strategies to the unique strengths and abilities of individual athletes, businesses can benefit from creating personalized experiences for their employees. Personalization in the workplace can lead to increased satisfaction, loyalty and overall success. In this chapter, we will explore various approaches to customizing employee experiences based on preferences and goals, as well as the impact of personalization on employee satisfaction and loyalty.

Approaches to Customizing Employee Experiences Based on Preferences and Goals

1. Personalized learning and development: Offer customized training and development programs that cater to each employee's unique learning preferences, strengths and areas of interest (Noe et al., 2017).
2. Flexible work arrangements: Provide options for flexible work hours, remote work or alternative

workspaces that accommodate individual preferences and work styles (Kossek et al., 2006).
3. Customized career paths: Develop tailored career plans that align with each employee's long-term goals and aspirations, providing opportunities for growth and advancement within the organization (Greenhaus et al., 2008).
4. Individualized feedback and performance evaluations: Provide personalized feedback and performance evaluations that take into account each employee's unique strengths, weaknesses and areas for improvement (Aguinis et al., 2012).

The Impact of Personalization on Employee Satisfaction and Loyalty

Personalization in the workplace has been shown to have a positive impact on employee satisfaction and loyalty, as it demonstrates the organization's commitment to meeting individual needs and fostering growth. Key benefits of personalization include:

1. Increased job satisfaction: Employees who feel their organization values their unique strengths and preferences are more likely to be satisfied with their jobs (Harter et al., 2002).
2. Enhanced loyalty: Personalized employee experiences contribute to increased loyalty and commitment to the organization, as employees perceive that their individual needs are being met and valued (Meyer et al., 2002).
3. Greater motivation and engagement: When employees feel that their organization is invested in their personal and professional growth, they are more

likely to be motivated and engaged in their work (Kahn, 1990).
4. Reduced turnover: Personalized employee experiences can lead to reduced turnover, as employees are more likely to remain with organizations that cater to their unique needs and preferences (Allen et al., 2004).

By embracing personalization in the workplace, businesses can create unique employee experiences that foster satisfaction, loyalty, and overall success, unlocking the power of sports to transform their organization.

Chapter 12

Recognition and Rewards: Celebrating Achievements and Milestones

Just as sports teams celebrate wins and individual achievements, businesses can benefit from recognizing and rewarding their employees' accomplishments. In this chapter, we will discuss effective systems for recognizing and rewarding employee accomplishments, as well as the influence of recognition and rewards on employee motivation.

Effective Systems for Recognizing and Rewarding Employee Accomplishments

1. Public recognition: Celebrate employee achievements in company meetings, newsletters or social media channels, fostering a sense of pride and accomplishment (Gostick & Elton, 2009).
2. Peer recognition programs: Implement programs that allow employees to recognize and celebrate their colleagues' achievements, fostering a culture of appreciation and support (Kessler, 2013).

3. Performance-based bonuses and incentives: Offer financial rewards tied to individual or team performance, encouraging employees to strive for excellence (Gerhart & Rynes, 2003).
4. Non-financial rewards: Provide non-monetary incentives such as flexible work hours, professional development opportunities or unique experiences to motivate and engage employees (Jeffrey, 2009).

The Influence of Recognition and Rewards on Employee Motivation

Recognition and rewards have been shown to have a significant impact on employee motivation. Key benefits of recognition and rewards include:

1. Increased motivation: Employees who feel their achievements are recognized and rewarded are more likely to be motivated to perform at their best (Brun & Dugas, 2008).
2. Enhanced performance: A well-designed recognition and rewards system can lead to improved employee performance, as employees are motivated to achieve specific goals (Shaw et al., 2002).
3. Greater job satisfaction: Employees who feel valued and appreciated for their efforts are more likely to be satisfied with their jobs (Harter et al., 2002).
4. Higher employee retention: Recognition and rewards can contribute to reduced turnover, as employees are more likely to remain with organizations that acknowledge and value their contributions (Allen et al., 2004).

By incorporating effective recognition and rewards systems,

businesses can celebrate their employees' achievements and milestones, unlocking the power of sports to transform their organization.

In summary, recognizing and rewarding employee accomplishments can lead to increased motivation, enhanced performance, greater job satisfaction and higher employee retention. By implementing effective systems for recognition and rewards, businesses can foster a culture of appreciation and support, ultimately unlocking the power of sports principles to transform their organization.

Chapter 13

Spectatorship: Learning and Growing Through Observation

In sports, spectatorship plays an important role in fostering a sense of community, supporting athletes and learning from their performance. Similarly, in the business world, providing opportunities for employees to observe and learn from their colleagues can foster a supportive and inspired workplace. In this chapter, we will discuss the opportunities for employees to observe and learn from their colleagues, as well as the role of spectatorship in fostering a supportive and inspired workplace.

Opportunities for Employees to Observe and Learn from Their Colleagues

1. Job shadowing: Encourage employees to shadow colleagues from other departments or with different roles to gain new perspectives and learn new skills (Hall, 2002).
2. Cross-functional teams: Create project teams composed of members from various departments to

facilitate collaboration, learning and the exchange of ideas (Griffin & Hauser, 1996).
3. Brown bag lunches and learning sessions: Organize informal meetings where employees can share their expertise, experiences and best practices with their colleagues (Garvin et al., 2008).
4. Collaborative tools and platforms: Implement tools and platforms that enable employees to share knowledge, ask questions and learn from each other in real-time (Stenmark, 2003).

The Role of Spectatorship in Fostering a Supportive and Inspired Workplace

Spectatorship in the workplace can provide employees with the following benefits:

1. Enhanced learning: Observing colleagues can help employees learn new skills, best practices and problem-solving approaches, contributing to their professional development (Bandura, 1977).
2. Increased motivation: Witnessing colleagues' achievements and progress can inspire employees to challenge themselves and strive for excellence (Locke & Latham, 2002).
3. Strengthened relationships: Sharing experiences and learning from one another can foster camaraderie, trust and a sense of belonging among employees (Wenger et al., 2002).

By creating opportunities for employees to observe and learn from their colleagues, businesses can foster a supportive and inspired workplace, where employees feel motivated and connected to their organization.

Part Three

The Sportified Company Certification and No1 Coaching

Chapter 14

The Sportified Company Certification: A Competitive Advantage

As businesses increasingly recognize the benefits of *Sportifying*, a new certification program has been developed to help organizations leverage these principles to gain a competitive edge. The Sportified Company Certification, pioneered by No1 Coaching, provides a framework for organizations to implement sports-inspired strategies and tactics in their workplace. In this chapter, we will discuss the certification process and criteria, as well as the benefits of becoming a certified Sportified Company.

Overview of the Certification Process and Criteria

The Sportified Company Certification process involves the following steps:

1. Assessment: Companies undergo a comprehensive assessment to evaluate their current practices and identify areas for improvement in line with Sportifying principles.
2. Training and Consultation: Organizations receive tailored training and consultation from No1 Coaching

experts to implement Sportifying strategies, such as promoting teamwork, fostering sportsmanship and implementing coaching and mentorship programs.
3. Implementation: Companies integrate Sportifying principles into their daily operations, with ongoing support from No1 Coaching.
4. Evaluation: After a designated period, organizations are evaluated on their adherence to Sportifying principles and the impact on business performance.
5. Certification: Companies that successfully meet the criteria and demonstrate a commitment to Sportifying principles receive the Sportified Company Certification.

Benefits of Becoming a Certified Sportified Company

By becoming a certified Sportified Company, organizations can enjoy several benefits, including:

1. Improved business performance: Companies that embrace Sportifying principles have been shown to experience increased productivity, employee engagement, and overall performance (Briner et al., 1997).
2. Enhanced employer branding: The Sportified Company Certification serves as a signal to potential employees, customers, and stakeholders that the organization values employee well-being, development, and engagement, making it an attractive place to work and do business with (Backhaus et al., 2002).
3. Access to a network of like-minded companies: Certified Sportified Companies can connect with

other organizations that share similar values and goals, facilitating knowledge sharing and collaboration.
4. Ongoing support and resources: Companies that achieve certification receive ongoing support from No1 Coaching, including access to resources, training and expert guidance.

By pursuing the Sportified Company Certification, organizations can demonstrate their commitment to Sportifying principles and gain a competitive advantage in the marketplace.

In conclusion, the Sportified Company Certification offers organizations a unique opportunity to improve their business performance and enhance their employer branding by embracing sports-inspired principles. By becoming a certified Sportified Company, organizations can join a growing community of like-minded companies committed to transforming their workplace through the power of Sportifying.

Chapter 15

No1 Coaching: Your Partner in Sportifying

In the pursuit of *Sportifying*, organizations need a trusted partner with expertise in implementing sports-inspired strategies and tactics. No1 Coaching, the pioneer of *Sportifying* and the Sportified Company Certification, is dedicated to helping businesses unlock the power of sports to transform their organizations. In this chapter, we will introduce No1 Coaching and its services and products, as well as how it can help organizations achieve *Sportifying* and the Sportified Company Certification.

Introduction to No1 Coaching and its Services and Products

No1 Coaching, founded by a team of experts with a passion for sports and business, offers a range of services and products designed to assist organizations in implementing Sportifying principles. These include:

1. Training and development programs: No1 Coaching provides tailored training programs for employees

and managers, focusing on teamwork, communication, skill development and leadership.
2. Coaching and mentorship: Expert coaches and mentors from No1 Coaching work with organizations to establish and enhance coaching and mentorship programs, providing guidance and support for employee growth.
3. Consulting services: No1 Coaching offers consulting services to help businesses integrate *Sportifying* principles into their operations, including strategies for promoting physical activity, fostering sportsmanship, and encouraging competition.
4. Sportified Company Certification: No1 Coaching administers the Sportified Company Certification process, working with organizations to assess, train and evaluate their commitment to Sportifying principles.

How No1 Coaching Can Help Organizations Achieve Sportifying and the Sportified Company Certification

No1 Coaching supports organizations in their Sportifying journey by:

1. Conducting thorough assessments to identify areas of improvement and develop tailored Sportifying strategies.
2. Providing expert guidance and support throughout the implementation process, ensuring that *Sportifying* principles are effectively integrated into the organization's daily operations.
3. Offering ongoing training, coaching and consulting services to maintain and enhance *Sportifying* efforts.

4. Administering the Sportified Company Certification process, evaluating organizations' progress and commitment to *Sportifying* principles.

By partnering with No1 Coaching, organizations can access the expertise, resources and support needed to effectively implement *Sportifying* strategies and work towards achieving the Sportified Company Certification.

In conclusion, No1 Coaching is the ideal partner for organizations seeking to leverage the power of sports to transform their workplace. Through its range of services and products, No1 Coaching provides the necessary guidance, training and support to help businesses unlock the benefits of *Sportifying* and achieve the Sportified Company Certification. By embracing *Sportifying* principles, organizations can enhance employee engagement, improve performance and gain a competitive advantage in today's fast-paced business environment.

Chapter 16

Conclusion - The Future of Sportifying and the Role of No1 Coaching

As we have explored throughout this book, Sportifying has the potential to revolutionize the way organizations approach employee engagement, performance and well-being. By adopting sports-inspired principles and strategies, businesses can create a more dynamic, collaborative, and motivated workforce. In this concluding chapter, we will look at the future of *Sportifying* in the business world and the role No1 Coaching will play in driving the *Sportifying* movement.

The Future of *Sportifying* in the Business World

The principles of *Sportifying* are only beginning to gain traction but their potential impact on the business world is significant. As more organizations recognize the benefits of *Sportifying* and embrace its concepts, we can expect to see several key trends emerging:

1. Increased focus on employee well-being: As businesses continue to prioritize employee health and wellness, *Sportifying* principles that promote physical

activity, teamwork and a supportive environment will become increasingly important (Grawitch et al., 2007).
2. Greater emphasis on continuous learning and development: Organizations that adopt *Sportifying* principles will increasingly invest in training and development programs, as well as coaching and mentorship initiatives, to help employees grow and succeed (Noe et al., 2017).
3. Shift towards personalized employee experiences: *Sportifying* concepts like adaptive difficulty, personalization and recognition will drive companies to create unique experiences that cater to individual employees' needs, preferences and goals (Peacock et al., 2018).
4. Strengthened employer branding: Businesses that embrace *Sportifying* will enhance their reputation as innovative, employee-centric organizations, attracting top talent and fostering loyalty (Backhaus et al., 2002).

The Role of No1 Coaching in Driving the Sportifying Movement

As the pioneer of *Sportifying* and the Sportified Company Certification, No1 Coaching is well-positioned to lead the charge in driving the *Sportifying* movement. The company will continue to play a vital role in promoting *Sportifying* principles by:

1. Offering comprehensive training, coaching and consulting services that help organizations successfully implement *Sportifying* strategies.
2. Expanding the Sportified Company Certification program to recognize and reward businesses that

demonstrate a strong commitment to *Sportifying* principles.
3. Conducting research and sharing knowledge on the benefits of *Sportifying*, furthering the understanding of its potential impact on the business world.
4. Building a global community of Sportified Companies, facilitating collaboration and knowledge-sharing among organizations that share a commitment to *Sportifying* principles.

In conclusion, the future of *Sportifying* in the business world is bright, with the potential to transform organizations and create more engaged, productive and satisfied workforces. As the driving force behind the *Sportifying* movement, No1 Coaching will continue to provide the expertise, resources and support necessary for businesses to unlock the power of sports-inspired principles and strategies. By embracing *Sportifying*, organizations can enhance their competitive advantage and contribute to a healthier, more dynamic business landscape.

Appendix 1: Conceptual Upgrades and Scaling Through Sportifying

Sportifying: Enhancing Gamification through Sports-Inspired Elements

Conceptual Upgrades:

1. Physicality: Introduce physical activity to the gamified system, encouraging users to engage their bodies and promote health and wellness. Examples include fitness tracking, motion controls and incorporating real-world activities.
2. Teamwork: Foster collaboration and communication among participants by promoting team-based challenges and goals. Encourage users to form teams, coordinate strategies and cooperate to achieve shared objectives.
3. Sportsmanship: Emphasize the importance of respect, fairness and integrity in the *sportified* system. Encourage participants to treat each other with dignity and adhere to ethical standards.

4. Skill Development: Integrate skill-building components that encourage users to learn and master new abilities, mirroring the progression and improvement seen in sports. Offer tutorials, training sessions and practice opportunities.
5. Competition: Incorporate healthy competition, such as tournaments, leagues and leaderboards to motivate users and create a sense of rivalry that can drive engagement and performance.
6. Adaptive Difficulty: Implement adaptive difficulty systems that automatically adjust the challenge level based on individual performance, ensuring that users remain engaged and challenged at an appropriate level.
7. Coaching and Mentorship: Offer coaching and mentorship opportunities, enabling experienced users to guide and support less experienced participants and fostering a culture of learning and growth. The coaching element helps to solve the extrinsic motivation problems found in gamification.
8. Personalization: Provide personalized experiences based on individual preferences, abilities and goals, tailoring the *sportified* system to each user's unique needs and aspirations.
9. Recognition and Rewards: Implement a system of recognition and rewards to celebrate user achievements, progress and milestones. Offer badges, trophies and other tangible symbols of accomplishment.
10. Spectatorship: Integrate spectator features, allowing users to watch and learn from the performance of others, fostering a sense of community and inspiration.

Terms and Definitions:

1. Sportifying: The process of enhancing gamification by incorporating elements from sports to improve engagement, motivation and skill development.
2. Physicality: The incorporation of physical activity and movement into a gamified system.
3. Teamwork: Collaboration and communication among participants to achieve shared goals and objectives.
4. Sportsmanship: Ethical behavior and respect among participants, including fairness, integrity and adherence to established rules.
5. Skill Development: The process of learning and mastering new abilities and techniques within a *sportified* system.
6. Adaptive Difficulty: A system that adjusts the challenge level based on individual performance to maintain engagement and provide an appropriate level of challenge.
7. Coaching and Mentorship: Opportunities for experienced users to guide and support less experienced participants, fostering a culture of learning and growth.
8. Personalization: Tailoring the *sportified* system to individual preferences, abilities, and goals to create unique and customized experiences.
9. Recognition and Rewards: Systems that acknowledge and celebrate user achievements, progress and milestones.
10. Spectatorship: Features that allow users to watch and learn from the performance of others, fostering a sense of community and inspiration.

Improvements:

1. Enhanced engagement through physical activity, competition and skill development.
2. Increased motivation due to team-based challenges, personalization and adaptive difficulty.
3. Improved overall user experience with a focus on sportsmanship, coaching and mentorship.
4. Fostering a culture of learning, growth and community through skill development and spectatorship.
5. Encouraging healthy behaviors, such as physical activity and collaboration that can translate to real-world benefits.

An Informal Guide to Sportifying for Business Growth and Scaling

Alright, now that we've covered the ins-and-outs of *Sportifying* in the previous chapters, let's dive into how it can help your business grow and scale. We're going to get a bit more informal here, so think of this as a friendly conversation about the real-life application of *Sportifying* principles.

1. Bringing Sportifying to Your Business Model

Robards, Stirling, and Milroy (2017) showed that combining sports and digital tech can create some pretty cool opportunities for businesses to generate revenue. So, why not think about how you can apply *Sportifying* principles to your own business model? Adding physical activity or some friendly competition to your products or services might be just the thing to keep customers coming back for more.

Key Takeaway: Get creative with how you can use *Sportifying* to pump up customer engagement and open up new revenue streams.

2. Getting Your Team Moving

We all know that a healthy workforce is a productive workforce. The *IO5 Manual for Gamification Methods in Physical Activity* has loads of ideas for getting people moving. Adapt some of these techniques for your workplace and watch your team's productivity skyrocket. And hey, healthier employees mean lower healthcare costs – that's a win-win for everyone!

Key Takeaway: Put some pep in your employees' steps with gamification techniques that promote wellness and watch the benefits roll in.

3. Riding the *Sportifying* Wave in the Game Industry

Sportifying has been a game-changer (pun intended) in the gaming industry, as highlighted by the Sport Tomorrow article. How about using *Sportifying* principles to create new products, services or marketing campaigns? With the right mix of sports excitement and digital engagement, you could have a winning formula for attracting customers and generating some serious buzz.

Key Takeaway: Don't be afraid to jump on the *Sportifying* bandwagon – it might be your ticket to standing out from the competition and boosting your revenue.

4. Learning from the World of Education

Rehm, Lupton, and Nielsen (2022) explored *Sportifying* in education but their insights can be useful for corporate training too. By adding *Sportifying* principles to employee training, you can create engaging learning experiences that lead to better skill development and knowledge retention. In the long run, this could help your business grow and scale.

Key Takeaway: Keep things interesting by injecting *Sportifying* into your employee training programs – who knows, it could be the secret to unlocking your company's full potential.

To wrap things up, *Sportifying* can be a powerful tool for boosting your business growth and scaling. By weaving these principles into your business model, promoting wellness, embracing *Sportifying* in product development and marketing and applying it to employee training, you can increase revenue, improve performance and set your business apart from the competition. So, why not give *Sportifying* a try? You might just find it's the game-changing strategy your business has been waiting for.

Appendix 2 – The Sportified Company Certification Program

Objective: The Sportified Company Certification Program aims to recognize and endorse organizations that effectively integrate Sportifying elements into their culture, products, services and operations. This certification provides companies with a competitive advantage and demonstrates their commitment to promoting employee engagement, motivation and overall well-being.

Certification Process:

1. Application: Companies interested in becoming a certified Sportified Company must complete an application form detailing their organization's information, *Sportifying* initiatives and supporting documentation.
2. Self-Assessment: Applicants are required to complete a comprehensive self-assessment based on the Sportified Company Certification Criteria (detailed below). This assessment should outline the specific

initiatives, strategies and achievements in each area of *Sportifying*.
3. Documentation: Submit supporting documents, such as policy documents, employee testimonials, internal reports and other relevant materials that showcase the company's commitment to *Sportifying*.
4. Evaluation: An independent panel of experts will review the application, self-assessment and supporting documentation. The panel may conduct interviews with company representatives, employees and other stakeholders to gather additional information.
5. Site Visit: A team of certification assessors may conduct a site visit to validate the information provided in the application and to evaluate the company's *Sportifying* initiatives in action.
6. Certification Decision: Based on the evaluation and site visit, the certification panel will make a decision on whether to award the Sportified Company Certification. Feedback and recommendations for improvement will be provided to the applicant, regardless of the decision.
7. Certification Maintenance: Certified Sportified Companies are required to submit annual reports demonstrating their ongoing commitment to *Sportifying* and continuous improvement. Periodic reassessments may be conducted to ensure compliance with certification criteria.

Appendix 2– The Sportified Company Certification Pro...

Sportified Company Certification Criteria:

1. Physicality: Demonstrate the integration of physical activity and wellness programs in the workplace, such as fitness facilities, workout classes, walking meetings or other initiatives that promote employee health.
2. Teamwork: Establish a culture of collaboration and communication, with opportunities for employees to engage in team-based activities, projects and challenges.
3. Sportsmanship: Foster an environment of respect, fairness and integrity among employees, with clear policies and guidelines for ethical behavior and conflict resolution.
4. Skill Development: Offer training and development programs to employees that focus on skill-building, personal growth and professional advancement.
5. Competition: Encourage healthy competition through events, contests and recognition systems that motivate employees to excel in their work and personal development.
6. Adaptive Difficulty: Implement systems and processes that cater to employees' individual skills, abilities, and goals, ensuring an appropriate level of challenge and engagement.
7. Coaching and Mentorship: Provide opportunities for experienced employees to guide and support less experienced colleagues, creating a culture of learning and growth.
8. Personalization: Customize employee experiences and development opportunities based on individual preferences, abilities and aspirations.

9. Recognition and Rewards: Establish recognition and reward systems that acknowledge employee achievements, progress and milestones.
10. Spectatorship: Create opportunities for employees to observe, learn from and support the achievements of their colleagues, fostering a sense of community and inspiration.

To "Sportify" the implementation of the Sportified Company Certification Program, we have introduced sports-inspired elements throughout the certification process, making it more engaging, competitive, and dynamic. Here are the stages of the certification process:

Application:

- We encourage companies to submit a creative video showcasing their *Sportifying* initiatives, engaging employees in the process and emphasizing their teamwork and sportsmanship.
- We offer early-bird incentives, like discounted application fees, to motivate applicants to apply promptly and create a sense of urgency, similar to registering for a sports event.

Self-Assessment:

- Our self-assessment is an interactive, gamified tool where companies can track their progress, unlock achievements and compare their scores with industry benchmarks or other applicants.
- We've included a dedicated section for companies to highlight their most innovative *Sportifying* initiatives, encouraging creativity and competition.

Documentation:

- Annually we host the *Sportified Championships*, a virtual and in-person event where applicants present their *Sportifying initiatives* to the certification panel and other companies, fostering collaboration, networking and learning from each other's experiences.

Evaluation:

- Our evaluation criteria is a transparent scoring system that evaluates companies based on their performance in each *Sportifying* criterion, encouraging competition and continuous improvement.
- We provide constructive feedback using sports coaching techniques to help companies identify areas for improvement and develop action plans to enhance their *Sportifying efforts*.

Site Visit:

- Our site visits act as a *Sportified Company Tour*, where employees act as guides, showcasing their *Sportifying initiatives* and sharing their experiences, fostering a sense of pride and ownership in the process.
- Site visits include team-building activities or mini-challenges during the site visit, allowing assessors to observe employees' teamwork, sportsmanship and skill development in action.

Certification Decision:

- Announce certification decisions at a virtual or in-person *Sportified Awards Ceremony*, celebrating the achievements of certified companies and fostering a sense of community and motivation.
- Offer tiered certifications (e.g., bronze, silver, gold) based on companies' *Sportifying scores*, encouraging continuous improvement and competition.

Certification Maintenance:

- We host annual *Sportified Summits* where certified companies can share best practices, network and learn from each other, fostering a sense of community and growth.
- We've introduced *Sportified Challenges*, periodic mini-competitions where certified companies can showcase their latest *Sportifying initiatives*, maintaining engagement and driving continuous improvement.

By incorporating these sports-inspired elements into the certification process, the Sportified Company Certification Program offers an example of a more engaging, motivating, and competitive experience that not only assesses companies' *Sportifying efforts* but also fosters a sense of community and growth among participants.

Bibliography

Allen, T. D., Eby, L. T., Poteet, M. L., Lentz, E., & Lima, L. (2004). Career benefits associated with mentoring for proteges: A meta-analysis. Journal of Applied Psychology, 89(1), 127-136.

Amabile, T. M., Conti, R., Coon, H., Lazenby, J., & Herron, M. (1996). Assessing the work environment for creativity. Academy of Management Journal, 39(5), 1154-1184.

Aguinis, H., & Kraiger, K. (2009). Benefits of training and development for individuals and teams, organizations, and society. Annual Review of Psychology, 60, 451-474.

Aguinis, H., Joo, H., & Gottfredson, R. K. (2012). Delivering effective performance feedback: The strengths-based approach. Business Horizons, 55(2), 105-111.

Backhaus, K., Stone, B. A., & Heiner, K. (2002). Exploring the relationship between corporate social performance and employer attractiveness. Business & Society, 41(3), 292-318.

Baicker, K., Cutler, D., & Song, Z. (2010). Workplace wellness programs can generate savings. Health Affairs, 29(2), 304-311.

Bandura, A. (1977). Social learning theory. Prentice-Hall.

Bock, L. (2015). Work Rules!: Insights from Inside Google That Will Transform How You Live and Lead. Hachette Books.

Brammer, S., Millington, A., & Rayton, B. (2007). The contribution of corporate social responsibility to organizational commitment. International Journal of Human Resource Management, 18(10), 1701-1719.

Briner, R. B., Denyer, D., & Rousseau, D. M. (2009). Evidence-based management: Concept cleanup time? Academy of Management Perspectives, 23(4), 19-32.

Brun, J. P., & Dugas, N. (2008). An analysis of employee recognition: Perspectives on human resources practices. The International Journal of Human Resource Management, 19(4), 716-730.

Carmeli, A., Brueller, D., & Dutton, J. E. (2009). Learning behaviours in the workplace: The role of high-quality interpersonal relationships and psychological safety. Systems Research and Behavioral Science, 26(1), 81-98.

Cerasoli, C. P., Nicklin, J. M., & Ford, M. T. (2014). Intrinsic motivation and extrinsic incentives jointly predict performance: A 40-year meta-analysis. Psychological Bulletin, 140(4), 980-1008.

de Haan, E., Duckworth, A., Birch, D., & Jones, C. (2013). Executive coaching outcome research: The contribution of common factors such as relationship, personality match, and self-efficacy. Consulting Psychology Journal: Practice and Research, 65(1), 40-57.

Deci, E. L., Kasser, T., & Ryan, R. M. (1999). The Relations of Need Satisfaction, Intrinsic Motivation, and Well-Being. Journal of Personality and Social Psychology, 76(3), 305-317.

Deci, E. L., Koestner, R., & Ryan, R. M. (1999). A meta-analytic review of experiments examining the effects of extrinsic rewards on intrinsic motivation. Psychological Bulletin, 125(6), 627–668.

Deci, E. L., & Ryan, R. M. (2008). Self-determination theory: A macrotheory of human motivation, development, and health. Canadian Psychology/Psychologie Canadienne, 49(3), 182–185.

Den Hartog, D. N., De Hoogh, A. H., & Belschak, F. D. (2013). Ethical leadership and subordinate outcomes: The mediating role of organizational commitment and the moderating role of power distance in the work unit. Journal of Business Ethics, 115(3), 667-680.

Deterding, S., Dixon, D., Khaled, R., & Nacke, L. (2011). From game design elements to gamefulness: defining "gamification." In Proceedings of the 15th International Academic MindTrek Conference (pp. 9-15). ACM.

Dirks, K. T., & Ferrin, D. L. (2002). Trust in leadership: Meta-analytic findings and implications for research and practice. Journal of Applied Psychology, 87(4), 611-628.

Doran, G. T. (1981). There's a S.M.A.R.T. way to write management's goals and objectives. Management Review, 70(11), 35-36.

Eby, L. T., Allen, T. D., Evans, S. C., Ng, T., & DuBois, D. L. (2013). Employing a multi-level approach to understanding the relationship between mentoring and career satisfaction. Journal of Vocational Behavior, 83(3), 376-387.

Edmondson, A. C. (2012). Teaming: How organizations learn, innovate, and compete in the knowledge economy. Jossey-Bass.

Edwards, M. (2019). The Power of Nike's Mission Statement: How a Well-Crafted Purpose Can Drive Business Success. Forbes.

Farzan, R., & Brusilovsky, P. (2011). Encouraging User Participation in a Course Recommender System: An Impact on User Behavior. Computers in Human Behavior, 27(1), 276-284.

Gagné, M., & Deci, E. L. (2005). Self-determination theory and work motivation. Journal of Organizational Behavior, 26(4), 331-362.

Bibliography

Gallup. (2017). State of the American Workplace. Retrieved from https://www.gallup.com/workplace/238085/state-american-workplace-report-2017.aspx

Garrett, G., Benden, M., Mehta, R., Pickens, A., Peres, S. C., & Zhao, H. (2016). Call center productivity over 6 months following a standing desk intervention. IIE Transactions on Occupational Ergonomics and Human Factors, 4(2-3), 188-195.

Garvin, D. A., Edmondson, A. C., & Gino, F. (2008). Is yours a learning organization? Harvard Business Review, 86(3), 109-116.

Gerhart, B., & Rynes, S. L. (2003). Compensation: Theory, evidence, and strategic implications. Sage Publications.

Gostick, A., & Elton, C. (2009). The Carrot Principle: How the Best Managers Use Recognition to Engage Their People, Retain Talent, and Accelerate Performance. Free Press.

Grawitch, M. J., Gottschalk, M., & Munz, D. C. (2006). The path to a healthy workplace: A critical review linking healthy workplace practices, employee well-being, and organizational improvements. Consulting Psychology Journal: Practice and Research, 58(3), 129-147.

Greenhaus, J. H., Callanan, G. A., & Godshalk, V. M. (2008). Career management. Sage Publications.

Griffeth, R. W., Hom, P. W., & Gaertner, S. (2000). A meta-analysis of antecedents and correlates of employee turnover: Update, moderator tests, and research implications for the next millennium. Journal of Management, 26(3), 463-488.

Griffin, A., & Hauser, J. R. (1996). Integrating R&D and marketing: A review and analysis of the literature. Journal of Product Innovation Management, 13(3), 191-215.

Hagen, M. (2012). Managerial coaching: A review of the literature. Performance Improvement Quarterly, 24(4), 17-39.

Hall, D. T. (2002). Careers in and out of organizations. Sage Publications.

Hamari, J., Koivisto, J., & Sarsa, H. (2014). Does Gamification Work? - A Literature Review of Empirical Studies on Gamification. In Proceedings of the 47th Hawaii International Conference on System Sciences (pp. 3025-3034). IEEE.

Hamer, M., & Chida, Y. (2008). Active commuting and cardiovascular risk: A meta-analytic review. Preventive Medicine, 46(1), 9-13.

Harter, J. K., Schmidt, F. L., & Hayes, T. L. (2002). Business-unit-level relationship between employee satisfaction, employee engagement, and business outcomes: A meta-analysis. Journal of Applied Psychology, 87(2), 268-279.

Hillman, C. H., Erickson, K. I., & Kramer, A. F. (2008). Be smart, exercise your heart: Exercise effects on brain and cognition. Nature Reviews Neuroscience, 9(1), 58-65.

Hülsheger, U. R., Anderson, N., & Salgado, J. F. (2009). Team-level predictors of innovation at work: A comprehensive meta-analysis spanning three decades of research. Journal of Applied Psychology, 94(5), 1128-1145.

Humphrey, S. E., Nahrgang, J. D., & Morgeson, F. P. (2007). Integrating motivational, social, and contextual work design features: A meta-analytic summary and theoretical extension of the work design literature. Journal of Applied Psychology, 92(5), 1332-1356.

Jeffrey, S. A. (2009). Justifiability and the motivational power of tangible noncash incentives. Human Performance, 22(2), 143-155.

Kahn, W. A. (1990). Psychological conditions of personal engagement and disengagement at work. Academy of Management Journal, 33(4), 692-724.

Kapp, K. M. (2012). The Gamification of Learning and Instruction: Game-based Methods and Strategies for Training and Education. John Wiley & Sons.

Kessler, S. R. (2013). The effects of on-the-job and informal learning on employee engagement. Human Resource Development Quarterly, 24(4), 501-525.

Klein, C., DiazGranados, D., Salas, E., Le, H., Burke, C. S., Lyons, R., & Goodwin, G. F. (2009). Does team building work? Small Group Research, 40(2), 181-222.

Kohn, A. (1992). No Contest: The Case Against Competition. Houghton Mifflin Harcourt.

Koivisto, J., & Hamari, J. (2019). The Rise of Motivational Information Systems: A Review of Gamification Research. International Journal of Information Management, 45, 191-210.

Kossek, E. E., Lautsch, B. A., & Eaton, S. C. (2006). Telecommuting, control, and boundary management: Correlates of policy use and practice, job control, and work–family effectiveness. Journal of Vocational Behavior, 68(2), 347-367.

Kim, S., Williams, R., & Rothstein, H. R. (2013). The effects of an organizational level sports-based intervention on workplace well-being. Journal of Workplace Behavioral Health, 28(2), 107-124.

Lacerenza, C. N., Marlow, S. L., Tannenbaum, S. I., & Salas, E. (2017). Team development interventions: Evidence-based approaches for improving teamwork. American Psychologist, 72(4), 366-379.

Landers, R. N., Auerbach, A. J., & Callan, R. C. (2017). Game-Based Training in the Modern Workplace: Practical Implications and Future Directions. In Gamification in Education and Business (pp. 341-355). Springer.

Locke, E. A., & Latham, G. P. (2002). Building a practically useful theory of goal setting and task motivation: A 35-year odyssey . American Psychologist, 57(9), 705-717.

Marsick, V. J., & Watkins, K. E. (2003). Demonstrating the value of an organization's learning culture: The dimensions of the learning organization questionnaire. Advances in Developing Human Resources, 5(2), 132-151.

Maurer, T. J. (2001). Career-relevant learning and development, worker age, and beliefs about self-efficacy for development. Journal of Management, 27(2), 123-140.

Mayer, D. M., Kuenzi, M., Greenbaum, R., Bardes, M., & Salvador, R. B. (2009). How low does ethical leadership flow? Test of a trickle-down model. Organizational Behavior and Human Decision Processes, 108(1), 1-13.

McGill, M. E., & Slocum Jr., J. W. (1998). A little leadership, please? Organizational Dynamics, 26(3), 39-49.

Meyer, J. P., Stanley, D. J., Herscovitch, L., & Topolnytsky, L. (2002). Affective, continuance, and normative commitment to the organization: A meta-analysis of antecedents, correlates, and consequences. Journal of Vocational Behavior, 61(1), 20-52.

Meyer, J. P., Becker, T. E., & Vandenberghe, C. (2004). Employee commitment and motivation: A conceptual analysis and integrative model. Journal of Applied Psychology, 89(6), 991-1007.

Mills, P. R., Kessler, R. C., Cooper, J., & Sullivan, S. (2007). Impact of a health promotion program on employee health risks and work productivity. American Journal of Health Promotion, (1), 45-53.

Morschheuser, B., Hamari, J., & Koivisto, J. (2016). Gamification in Crowdsourcing: A Review. In Proceedings of the 49th Hawaii International Conference on System Sciences (pp. 4375-4384). IEEE.

Murayama, K., & Elliot, A. J. (2012). The competition–performance relation: A meta-analytic review and test of the opposing processes model of competition and performance. Psychological Bulletin, 138(6), 1035-1070.

Nacke, L. E., & Deterding, S. (2017). The maturing of gamification research. Computers in Human Behavior, 71, 450-454.

Nicholson, S. (2015). A RECIPE for Meaningful Gamification. In Gamification in Education and Business (pp. 1-20). Springer.

Noe, R. A. (1999). Employee training and development. Irwin/McGraw-Hill.

Noe, R. A., Clarke, A. D., & Klein, H. J. (2014). Learning in the twenty-first-century workplace. Annual Review of Organizational Psychology and Organizational Behavior, 1, 245-275.

Noe, R. A., Clarke, A. D., & Klein, H. J. (2017). Learning in the twenty-first-century workplace. Annual Review of Organizational Psychology and Organizational Behavior, 4, 245-269.

Nyberg, A. J., Moliterno, T. P., Hale, D., & Lepak, D. P. (2010). Resource-based perspectives on unit-level human capital: A review and integration. Journal of Management, 36(1), 163-191.

Oppezzo, M., & Schwartz, D. L. (2014). Give your ideas some legs: The positive effect of walking on creative thinking. Journal of Experimental Psychology: Learning, Memory, and Cognition, 40(4), 1142-1152.

Parker-Wilkins, V. (2006). Business impact of executive coaching: Demonstrating monetary value. Industrial and Commercial Training, 38(2), 70-77.

Pelletier, K. R. (2005). A review and analysis of the clinical and cost-effectiveness studies of comprehensive health promotion and disease management programs at the worksite: Update VII 2004–2008. Journal of Occupational and Environmental Medicine, 47(10), 1051-1058.

Pink, D. H. (2009). Drive: The Surprising Truth About What Motivates Us. Riverhead Books.

Prendergast, C. (1999). The provision of incentives in firms. Journal of Economic Literature, 37(1), 7-63.

Pronk, N. P. (2015). Placing workplace wellness in proper context: Value beyond money. Preventing Chronic Disease, 12, E127.

Raybourn, E. M. (2014). A New Paradigm for Serious Games: Transmedia Learning for More Effective Training and Education. Journal of Computational Science, 5(3), 471-481.

Rigby, S., & Ryan, R. M. (2011). Glued to Games: How Video Games Draw Us In and Hold Us Spellbound. Praeger.

Rock, D., & Donde, R. (2008). Driving organizational change with internal coaching programs: Part one. Industrial and Commercial Training, 40(1), 10-18.

Roepke, A. M., Jaffee, S. R., Riffle, O. M., & McGonigal, J. (2015). Randomized Controlled Trial of SuperBetter, a Smartphone-Based/Internet-Based Self-Help Tool to Reduce Depressive Symptoms. Games for Health Journal, 4(3), 235-246.

Ryan, R. M., & Deci, E. L. (2000). Self-determination theory and the facilitation of intrinsic motivation, social development, and well-being. American Psychologist, 55(1), 68–78.

Sailer, M., Hense, J., Mandl, H., & Klevers, M. (2013). Psychological perspectives on motivation through gamification. Interaction Design and Architecture(s) Journal, 19, 28-37.

Sailer, M., Hense, J. U., Mayr, S. K., & Mandl, H. (2017). How Gamification Motivates: An Experimental Study of the Effects of Specific Game Design Elements on Psychological Need Satisfaction. Computers in Human Behavior, 69, 371-380.

Saks, A. M., & Haccoun, R. R. (2010). Managing performance through training and development. Nelson Education.

Salas, E., Sims, D. E., & Burke, C. S. (2005). Is there a "big five" in teamwork? Small Group Research, 36(5), 555-599.

Salas, E., Cooke, N. J., & Rosen, M. A. (2008). On teams, teamwork, and team performance: Discoveries and developments. Human Factors, 50(3), 540-547.

Seaborn, K., & Fels, D. I. (2015). Gamification in Theory and Action

Shaw, J. D., Gupta, N., & Delery, J. E. (2002). Pay dispersion and workforce performance: Moderating effects of incentives and interdependence. Strategic Management Journal, 23(6), 491-512.

Stenmark, D. (2003). Knowledge sharing in organizations: Comparing two alternative incentive systems. 9th European Conference on Information Technology Evaluation (ECITE 2002), 791-798.

Tauer, J. M., & Harackiewicz, J. M. (2004). The effects of cooperation and competition on intrinsic motivation and performance. Journal of Personality and Social Psychology, 86(6), 849-861.

Tharenou, P., Saks, A. M., & Moore, C. (2007). A review and critique of research on training and organizational-level outcomes. Human Resource Management Review, 17(3), 251-273.

Tews, M. J., Michel, J. W., & Allen, D. G. (2013). Fun and friends: The impact of workplace fun and constituent attachment on turnover in a hospitality context. Human Relations, 66(8), 1027-1050.

Treviño, L. K., Butterfield, K. D., & McCabe, D. L. (1998). The ethical context in organizations: Influences on employee attitudes and behaviors. Business Ethics Quarterly, 8(3), 447-476.

Treviño, L. K., Weaver, G. R., & Reynolds, S. J. (2006). Behavioral ethics in organizations: A review. Journal of Management, 32(6), 951-990.

Treviño, L. K., Hartman, L. P., & Brown, M. (2000). Moral person and moral manager: How executives develop a reputation for ethical leadership. California Management Review, 42(4), 128-142.

Wenger, E. C., McDermott, R. A., & Snyder, W. M. (2002). Cultivating communities of practice: A guide to managing knowledge. Harvard Business School Press.

Made in the USA
Columbia, SC
09 February 2024